Gracious Heavenly Father

Gracious Heavenly Father

A Collection of Morning Prayers

Stacy L. Sanchez

Gracious Heavenly Father:
A Collection of Morning Prayers

By Stacy L. Sanchez

Scripture taken from the *Holy Bible*, New Living Translation, copyright © 1996, 2004, 2015 by Tyndale House Foundation. Used by permission of Tyndale House Publishers, Inc., Carol Stream, Illinois 60188. All rights reserved.

Cover Photo: Stacy L. Sanchez

ISBN: 978-1-7326327-4-5

Gracious Heavenly Father,

How majestic You are.

You paint the sky
in darkness,
sprinkled with stars,
then, oh so gently,
one ray of
sunlight after another,
You usher in daylight,
and the hope of a new beginning.

With you,
each day
is a new beginning.

With you,
each moment
overflows with hope.

You are the Light of the world.

You dispel darkness.

May Your love
shine bright
in me today.

Together,
may we dispel
darkness
and oh, so gently,
one ray of
hope after another,
usher in Godlight,
illuminating this world
with the light of Your love.

In Jesus' precious name,
I pray.

Amen.

Gracious Heavenly Father,

I pray that You
would
stand guard today.

Stand guard over my mouth.

Let only that
which is
edifying,
uplifting,
and truthful
flow from my mouth
and into the ears of others.

Stand guard over my heart.

Let only that
which is
truthful,
helpful
and of You
flow from the mouth of others
and into my heart.

Stand guard over my life.

Let only that
which is
blessed by Your hand
flow from the world
and into my life.

Stand guard over my calling.
Let only that
which is
building Your kingdom
flow from my life
and into the world.

In Jesus' precious name,
I pray.

Amen.

Gracious Heavenly Father,

Help me to be still, Lord.

To listen hard
for the voice
of Your Spirit.

In the busyness
of my day,
and the rush
to be and do,
may I still
undeniably,
unmistakably,
hear the hush
of Your Spirit.

Sometimes, Lord,
You speak in the power
of the whirlwind.

Sometimes, Father God,
Your voice is as loud
as the thunder.

But most times,
Precious Spirit,
Your voice comes
as a whisper
to a listening soul.

A soft stirring.

A gentle nudging.

A tender prodding.

A quiet conviction.

No matter how loud
the world may be,
no matter how many voices
vie for my attention,
may it be Your voice
I hear, Father God,

Your voice I listen to,
Your voice I follow.

Help me to be still, Lord.

To listen hard
for the voice
of Your Spirit.

In Jesus' precious name,
I pray.

Amen.

Gracious Heavenly Father,

Thank you for choosing
to abide with me.

With the presence
of Your precious Holy Spirit,
I am never alone.

Never alone in my weakness.

Never alone in my fear.

Never alone in my sorrow.

Never alone in my suffering.

Never alone in my thoughts.

Never alone in my abilities.

Never alone in my tasks.

Never alone in my responsibilities.

Never alone in my decision making.

Never alone in my coming and going.

Never alone in my calling.

Never alone in my living.

Never alone in myself.

You are here.

You are with me.
You are before me.
You are behind me.
You are beside me.
You are among me.
You are WITHIN me.

Thank you, Father.

To be indwelled with Your Spirit,
to never be
out of Your care,
out of Your sight,
out of Your presence -
what a precious gift,
what amazing peace,
what a beautiful God You are.

I praise You, Father.

I rejoice in Your companionship.

I delight in Your love.

I marvel at such a God as You.

In Jesus' precious name,
I pray.

Amen.

Gracious Heavenly Father,

As I sit in the stillness
and the newness of
this never lived before day,
I hear the praise of Your creation.

Floating though the window,
a melody unlike any other,
a symphony of tweets and chirps
fills my ears.

Oh, Lord,
may my heart
be as that
of these feathered friends.

May each morning,
my heart and my lips
erupt in praise to You.

May I awake with a song of praise
bursting forth from deep inside of me,
and may I sing Your praise all day long.

Oh, Father God,
how beautifully wonderful You are.
how majestic and mighty,
how tender and compassionate,
how strong and powerful,

how intimate and personal,
how holy and just,
how caring and kind.

Oh, Lord, I praise You.
With every fiber of my being,
I praise You.

May my praise,
like the songs of praise
filling my yard,
fill my home,
fill my neighborhood,
fill my work environment,
fill my city,
fill my country,
fill my world,
with praise to YOU.

In Jesus' precious name,
I pray.

Amen.

Gracious Heavenly Father,

A new day is before me,
and with it comes
demands and deadlines,
tasks to be accomplished
and needs to be supplied.

The Lord is my shepherd,
I lack nothing.

As I go through
the hustle and bustle
of doing this,
taking care of that,
planning ahead and
finishing up from behind,
I will keep my thoughts on You
and Your peace will be with me.

He makes me lie down in green pastures,
he leads me beside quiet waters,
he refreshes my soul.

As I decide on this,
and ponder that,
as I am faced with
challenges,

possible deadends,
seemingly insurmountable obstacles,
I will trust You
and Your leading in my life.

He guides me along the right paths
for his name's sake.
Even though I walk
through the darkest valley,
I will fear no evil,
for you are with me;
your rod and your staff,
they comfort me.

No matter what may happen,
no matter what may come my way,
no matter how hard the task
or how sweet the blessing,
I will praise You in and through it all.

You prepare a table before me
in the presence of my enemies.
You anoint my head with oil;
my cup overflows.

You are my God
and You have created this day.

You are with me in it.

You are with me through it.

You are with me despite it.

You are with me
working all things
for my good and Your glory.

I praise You, Father God.

Surely your goodness and love
will follow me
all the days of my life,
and I will dwell
in the house of the Lord
forever.

Thank you for today, Lord.

Thank you for what
You are doing
and for what
You have already done.

Thank you for all that lies ahead.

Thank you for
guiding and leading,
providing and protecting,
shielding and defending,
supplying and accompanying,
abiding and blessing.

In Jesus' precious name,
I pray.

Amen.

*Based on Psalms 23

Gracious Heavenly Father,

As I sit in the stillness
of a brand new day,
my heart rejoices
that You are here with me.

Not just in this
time and space,
but in those
yet to come.

Not just in this
stillness,
but in the unstill moments
still ahead.

Not just in this
new day,
but in the very heart
of this new creation.

Oh, Father God, -
You who know
no time or space,

You who whisper
to my heart
"Be still, and know that I am God",

You who make
all things new,

consume me
with Your Spirit today.

Anoint me with the oil of Your gladness.

Touch me with the healing of Your hands.

Cleanse me with the fire of Your Word.

Fill me with the power of Your presence.

Lead me with the voice of Your Spirit.

Consume me
so all that is left
of me
is You.

I give this moment to You, Lord.
I give this day to You, Lord.

I give this heart to You, Lord.
I give this life to You, Lord.

Take it - all of it -
and make it Yours.

Take it - all of it -
and use it
for Your good pleasure.

Take it - all of it -
and bring glory
to You through it.

Take it - all of it -
and accept it
as my sacrifice to You.

In Jesus' precious name,
I pray.

Amen.

Gracious Heavenly Father,

How I lift Your name on high.

You,
always faithful,
always kind,
always merciful,
God.

You,
who know
me better
than my dearest loves,
love me the dearest
and the best.

You,
who know
all my hidden thoughts
and secret doings,
love me with a love
that is showcased to all.

You,
who know
when I fall,
when I fail,

love me yet,
still,
and in spite of.

You,
who know
my love is fickle
and sometimes withheld,
love me with a love
that is unstoppable.

Oh, Lord.
my heart almost can't comprehend
a love like Yours, -
a love so pure,
a love so true,
a love so unconditional and never-ending.

And yet,
somehow,
deep down in my spirit,
I know Your love,
a love too good to be true,
is so very true.

I have seen it.

I have felt it.

I have received it.

I have been
restored
and redeemed
by it.

Only Your love, Lord,
could stoop so very low
and lift so very high.

Forgive me, Father God.

Teach me
to love You
as You so beautifully
love me.

In Jesus' precious name,
I pray.

Amen.

Gracious Heavenly Father,

A new day is dawning,
and it's time to wake up -
to the new thing You are doing,
to the new person You are creating in me,
to the new desire You
have placed in my heart,
to the new life You have called me into.

Lord,
Sometimes,
I feel like I'm living my life asleep.

Sometimes,
I don't notice Your blessings,
I don't harken to Your voice,
I don't respond to your Spirit,
I don't move to the beat of Your heart.

I lazily, lollygag through my day,
unaware,
unresponsive,
unmoved,
unchanged.

Wake me up, Father God.

Pull off the blankets
of complacency.

Flip on the light
of abundant,
God-filled living.

Take hold of my heart
and help me
step out of my sleep
and step out into
true life
found only in You.

I don't want to live my life
"sleep walking", Lord.

I want to be
fully awake,
fully alive,
fully FULL of You.

In Jesus' precious name,
I pray.

Amen.

Gracious Heavenly Father,

As I sit and meditate
upon Your goodness,
I am filled
with joy.

As I sit and ponder
Your power and might,
I am filled
with courage and strength.

As I sit and contemplate
Your wisdom,
I am filled
with peace.

As I sit and marvel at
Your mercy, grace, and love,
I am filled
with thankfulness,
humility,
and love
of my own.

As I sit and be still,
I know YOU are God.

This knowing -
this knowing YOU,
fills me with ALL of You
and makes me whole.

Thank you, Lord.

In Jesus' precious name,
I pray.

Amen.

Gracious Heavenly Father,

As I pour out
my heart before You,
I don't even know
where to begin
or how all of this
 is going to end.

My child,
I am the Alpha and Omega,
the beginning and the end.

I've got this and I've got you.

The voice of the world,
the cry of my heart,
and Your still, small voice -
all intertwined together,
a muffled, muting combination.

How can I hear You, Lord?

How can I find You
 in all of this,
Father God?

My child,
my word is a lamp for your feet
and a light for your path.

My Spirit will lead you into all truth.

I am The Way, The Truth, and The Life.

Ask, and you will receive.
Seek, and you will find.
Knock, and the door will be opened to you.

I am here,
in the midst of all the confusion,
and you will find me
when you search for me
with all of your heart.

Oh, Father God,
I am weary of the battle,
weary of the fight.

I long for peace,
calm assurance,
unending strength.

My child,
My peace I give to you.

Not as the world gives peace,
for my peace passes all understanding.

I am not the author of confusion,
I am truth.

Truth you can stake your very life on.

Rest in my faithfulness,
walk in my strength.

Your will, Abba Father,
This is where I want to be.

Your plan, loving Lord,
This is want I desire most.

Your obedient child, Heavenly Father,
This is who I want to be.

My child,
I know the desires of your heart.

If you will but delight yourself in me,
I will grant them all.

I love you, my child.

I always have and I always will.

I am here.

Be at peace.

Thank you, Father God.

In Jesus' precious name,
I pray.

Amen.

Gracious Heavenly Father,

I long to be
an instrument of You,
a vessel of honor
to be used by You,

but first, Father God,
teach me to love.

In Jesus' precious name,
I pray.

Amen.

Gracious Heavenly Father,

Open the eyes
of my heart
to see You more.

To see You when
 blessings abound.

To see You when
darkness surrounds.

To see You when
no one else is around.

To see You when
You just can't seem
to be found.

Open the eyes
of my heart
to feel You more.

To feel You when
my joy is full.

To feel You when
my strength is null.

To feel You when
life is wonderful.

To feel You when
my faith grows dull.

Open the eyes
of my heart
to know You more.

To know You are always here.

To know You are always near.

To know You hold me dear.

To know, with You, I shall not fear.

I want to
see You,
feel You,
know You.

Please Father God,
Open the eyes of my heart
and reveal YOU
in every situation,
in every circumstance,

in every moment,
in every day.

In Jesus' precious name,
I pray.

Amen.

Gracious Heavenly Father,

You want nothing more
than for Your child
to walk in truth.

So often, though,
I feel as though
I am in a game
of hide-n-seek with You.

I feel as though
I somehow
have to make my way
through a maze of
"this way" or "that way"
in order to find
my way to You.

I wonder why
knowing Your will
and finding Your way
is so hard to do.

And yet, the truth is this:

You are not hiding;
I am not truly seeking.

You are not silent;
I am not truly listening.

You are not ducking and dodging
in an effort to stay
one step out of touch with me;
I am not zeroing in and focusing
totally and completely
on You.

The problem is not with You, Father God.
(Never has been. Never will be.)

The problem is with me.
(Always.)

I allow everything and everyone
to overshadow and drown out
what You are doing,
what You are saying,
what You are guiding me to
or leading me through.

I remember Peter, Lord.

How, walking on the water,
You held out your hand

and invited Peter
to walk to You
and with You.

Stepping out of the boat,
eyes, ears, and faith
all completely on You, Jesus,
it was easy for him
to know what to do,
where to step,
which direction to go.

And do, step, and go, he did.

Right on top of the water,
right straight to You,
until......

Oh, Father God,
this is the word
(and the moment!)
that always causes me
to stumble,
to fall,
to doubt,
to become fearful and confused.

I hear You calling.

I sense Your leading.

I know what You are
calling me to
and I am willing
to do, step, and go

until.....

until I am reminded about this,
until I start to realize that,
until I listen to them,
until I forget about,
until I TAKE. MY. EYES. OFF. OF. YOU.

Help me, Father God
in my "until" moments.

Help me to keep
seeking You with all my heart.

Help me to keep
listening to Your still small voice.

Help me to keep
removing all that blocks
my view of You.

Help me to keep
stepping out,

placing one foot of my faith
in front of the other
UNTIL
I reach You, Lord.

Oh, Father God,
You want nothing more
than for Your child
to walk in truth.

You will be faithful
to lead me,
if only,
I will be faithful
to follow.

Thank you, Father God.

In Jesus' precious name,
I pray.

Amen.

Gracious Heavenly Father,

Once again
You have blessed me with
another day,
another moment,
another breath.

Oh Father God,
may I not
take this gift for granted.

May I not
grumble or complain.

May I not
misspend or misuse
one moment.

May each moment,
each breath,
be spent
shouting Your praises,
building Your kingdom,
accomplishing Your will,
all. day. long.

Thank you for the gift of today, Father.

I place it back
in Your hands, Lord,
to be lived as You see fit -
a humble sacrifice
from a thankful heart.

In Jesus' precious name,
I pray.

Amen.

Gracious Heavenly Father,

The Giver of all good gifts,
I thank you for the gift of today.

As I yawn and stretch
and try to wake up,
I feel the excitement
of all this day holds.

Nothing special
on my calendar.

No grandiose plans
or black-tie events.

And yet I know,
this day
will be amazing.

For you, Father God,
have already
mapped it
out for me.

For you, my precious Abba Father,
have lovingly
tucked blessings

into each nook
and each cranny of it.

For you, my strength and my Redeemer,
have smoothed the way
and have gone before.

For you, my friend and faithful companion,
are here,
walking beside me
to cheer me up
and cheer me on.

I can't wait

to see Your heartprints,

to hear Your still small voice,

to taste of Your goodness,

to smell the fragrance of Your love,

to feel Your very presence,

in all I do,
every place I go,
every minute of the day,
all day long.

Thank you, Lord.

You. are. my. life.
and for this
I give
unending thanks.

In Jesus' precious name,
I pray.

Amen.

Gracious Heavenly Father,

You alone know

the number of hairs
on my head,

the thoughts that run wild
through my mind,

the deepest longings of my heart.

You alone hear

the silent whisper
of my soul,

the quiet cry
of my heart,

the unspoken words
of my innermost being.

It is You,
and You alone.

As I go through this day,
may it be
You alone
guiding me,
leading me,
teaching me,
molding me,
changing me.

Let me not get tangled up in
the voice of the world,
the voice of the enemy,
the voice of my own selfish heart.

Let me hear You,
and You alone.

Let me follow You,
and You alone.

Let me honor You
and You alone.

In Jesus' precious name,
I pray.

Amen.

Gracious Heavenly Father,

As I live out this day,
the desire of my heart
is to be present
in Your presence.

No matter where I may go,
no matter what I may do,
no matter who may surround me,
no matter how this day unfolds,
no matter when everything and everyone
vies for my attention –
I desire to be present
in Your presence.

For you are here, Lord,
always and forever.

You are as close
as the whisper
of Your name.

You are alive in me,
filling me,
strengthening me,
directing me,
correcting me,
protecting me,

re-creating me,
blessing me,
communing with me.

Don't let me miss
one glimpse
 of You, Lord.

Don't let me miss
one word
from You, Lord.

Don't let me miss
one touch
from You, Lord.

To be present
in Your presence,
moment by moment,
all day long –

this is the desire of my heart.

Thank you, Lord,
for choosing
to be present
with me.

In Jesus' precious name,
I pray.

Amen.

Gracious Heavenly Father,

How my heart rejoices
to sing Your praise.

You know me better
than I know myself, -
intimately,
personally,
passionately,
faithfully.

You love me better
than I love myself, -
completely,
unselfishly,
unconditionally,
faithfully.

How can I ever doubt
Your presence in my life?

How can I ever doubt
Your goodness in my life?

How can I ever doubt You?

For You, oh God, are forever faithful.

And me,
I am forever yours.

Thank you, Lord.

In Jesus' precious name,
I pray.

Amen.

Gracious Heavenly Father,

Ruler of the Universe,
rule in my heart today.

When decisions arise,
and choices come,
let all I choose,
glorify You.

When thoughts are formed,
and words are spoken,
let all I say,
glorify You.

When fear shows up,
and temptation barges in,
let all I resist,
glorify You.

When the world needs me,
and "self" is required,
let all I give,
glorify You.

When You look upon your servant,
and gaze into my heart,
let all that I am,
glorify You.

In Jesus' precious name,
I pray.

Amen.

Gracious Heavenly Father,

Help me to keep my focus.

It's so easy
to get
blinded by the world,

to get
sucked into
worrying about what doesn't matter,
talking about what doesn't matter,
wasting time and energy
doing what doesn't matter.

Lord, help me to stay true to my mission.

You have called me
to be a child of light.

You have called me
to be salt on this earth.

Too often,
I simply disappear
into the crowd.

Too often,
I succumb
to being like the world.

Too often,
I as Your child,
grumble and complain,
gossip and backbite,
seek the approval of others,
serve self and self alone.

Remind me
of who
I am in you.

Remind me
of who
You have called me to be.

Remind me
it is not
about me,
it is about You.

Set me free
from a worldly mentality
that I might live
each moment of each day
with a spiritual intentionality.

Forgive me, Lord.

Empower me, Lord.

Surround me, Lord.

Change me, Lord.

In Jesus precious name,
I pray.

Amen.

Gracious Heavenly Father,

How beautiful You are.

Daily You fill me
to overflowing
with blessings
too numerous
to count.

Sunshine!
Air to breathe!
Safety as I go about my day!
Your constant companionship!
Trials!
Heartaches!
Sufferings!

Yes,
in all of these,
there is a blessing
to be found.

Anything that brings me
running to You,

anything that causes me
to direct my thoughts to You,

anything that draws me
closer to You,

good or bad,
happy or sad,

can be counted a blessing.

Give me eyes of faith, God.

Give me a heart
that runs to You, Father.

Give me hands
that willing receive,
firmly believing,
always knowing,
YOU are the true blessing
in the midst of it all.

In Jesus' precious name,
I pray.

Amen.

Gracious Heavenly Father,

To give thanks
in ALL things.

ALL things.

The good, the bad,
the happy, the sad.

Sometimes,
It's a struggle.

A battle.

A knock-down-drag out-fight.

And yet,
I know this truth:

You are in ALL things.

You are at work in ALL things.

You see
and You know
and You love –

ALL the time.

Father,
give me the strength
to surrender
everything in my life
to You
in a spirit of thanksgiving,
as a sacrifice of praise.

Forgive me, Father God,
for the times
"Thank you, Lord"
doesn't
come easy
from my lips
or my heart.

Forgive me for the times
I fail to recognize
Your faithfulness,
Your mercy,
and Your grace
in every situation,
in every circumstance,
in every trial,
in every tear.

Oh, Father God,
how could I not
offer You thanksgiving?

How could I not
be thankful?

For you, Oh Lord,
are holy and just,
compassionate and kind,
beautiful
beyond words.

Thank you, Abba Father.

Thank you, Almighty God.

Thank you, Jesus.

May my life
always overflow
in thanksgiving
to You.

In Jesus' precious name,
I pray.

Amen.

Gracious Heavenly Father,

Only You
could orchestrate
a new day to follow night,
new hope to follow despair,
new joy to follow sorrow,
new life to follow death.

As I go through this day,
keep my focus on the "new"
found only in You.

May the
hardships,
trials,
and disappointments of life
never dim
my vision of You,
but rather,
may they always
bring You
to the forefront
of my heart.

May they always be
a reminder
to me

of Your
strength,
peace,
presence,
and faithfulness
in my life.

May these
light afflictions
keep me
pressing on
and pressing deeper
into You
in search of the "new"
You have promised.

Through it all,
may these be
the very things
by which I come
to know You
in a new,
deeper,
more personal way.

In Jesus' precious name,
I pray.

Amen.

Gracious Heavenly Father,

You are
so kind
and merciful
in all of Your ways;
perfect
in all that You do.

Knowing this,
remembering this,
allowing this
to settle deep
in my heart
and take root, -
this is the way
I can praise You
in spite of,
in the midst of,
even though.

It's not that
my circumstances
are always praise worthy,
You are.

It's not that
my situations
are always good,

You are.

It's not that
I am choosing
to go through life
with rose-colored glasses on
oblivious to the
heartache,
pain,
and trials.

It's that I
am choosing
to go through life
with my eyes
securely fixed on You.

It's that I
am always praying
to see
Your heart,
Your purpose,
Your die-for-me love,
through each tear drop,
alongside each step,
woven through each moment.

Help me not to focus
on the "what" of my life,

but the "who" –

You,
my gracious, Heavenly Father -
so kind
and merciful
in all Your ways;
perfect
in all
that You do.

In Jesus' precious name,
I pray.

Amen.

Gracious Heavenly Father,

How amazing to think,
You,
who know all things,
know me.

You know my weaknesses.

You feel my insecurities.

You understand my fears.

You comprehend
the deepest desires
of my heart.

All my failures,
all my worries,
all my dreams,
all of me.

In a world
where I am sometimes
misunderstood,
mistaken,
misrepresented,
misjudged,
You know me.

Inside and out,
backwards and forward,
then and now,
all of me.

Just to know
that You know
brings
such comfort and hope.

To be known
by The One
who truly knows,
what a gift.

May I come
to know You, too.

In Jesus' precious name,
I pray.

Amen.

Gracious Heavenly Father,

Once again,
You have
generously
given me a new day
and have opened my eyes
to a new sunrise.

You have started me out
fresh and clean
with mercies
as new
as this day.

Oh, Father God-
may this day
be unlike any day
I have ever
lived before.

May this day
truly find me
walking in Your Spirit,
living in Your will,
practicing Your presence,
keenly aware of You
in every moment
of my day.

May I not let
worry or concern
steal my
peace
in You.

May I not let
criticism or judgment
steal my
joy
in You.

May I not let
selfishness or self talk
steal my
wisdom
in You.

May I not let
fear or unbelief
steal my
victory
in You.

May I not let
vanity or pride
steal my
reliance
in You.

Oh, Father God–
may I not waste
one moment
of this day
living apart
from You.

Thank you, Lord.

I love You
and praise You!

I can't wait
to live
this day
in Your presence.

In Jesus' precious name,
I pray.

Amen.

Gracious Heavenly Father,

Everywhere I look,
I see
turmoil and tension,
except
when I look
to You.

Everywhere I look,
I see
evil running rampant,
except
 when I look
to You.

Everywhere I look,
I see
chaos and corruption,
except
when I look
to You.

Everywhere I look,
I see
hopelessness and despair,
except
when I look
to You.

Lord,
help me
to keep my eyes
on You.

But, Lord,
I also pray that
through my words,
through my actions,
through my life,
through my very day to day
living of each day,
I might lift You high,
so others
may look upon You, too,
and find the
joy,
righteousness,
peace,
and hope
I find in You.

In Jesus' precious name,
I pray.

Amen.

Gracious Heavenly Father,

How beautiful You are.

From one
sunrise to the next,
You are faithful.

Unchanging God.

May my heart
become like Yours.

Steadfast.

Loyal.

Rock Solid.

May my love
for You
be as constant as
each sunrise,
each sunset.

May my pursuit of You
match Your pursuit of me –

unrelenting,

unending,

unequaled.

In Jesus' precious name,
I pray.

Amen.

Gracious Heavenly Father,

You are knowledgeable
about all things;
I, Your child,
am not.

You know the end
from the beginning,
and all in between;
I, Your child,
do not.

You can see the ins and outs,
the orchestrating of details;
I, Your child,
can not.

You alone are wisdom.

You alone are truth.

Lord,
it is not
in the way of man
to direct
his own steps.

I,
who only see
here and now,
bits and pieces,
this and that
cannot see clearly

the way to go,

the choices to make,

the direction to head.

You alone know.

So,
I come to You,
Father God,
asking You
to lead me.

I want only to be
in Your will,
to follow Your path,
to walk the way
You would have me
to travel.

As I seek You
above all else,
help me,
Your child,
to hear
Your still small voice
above
the noise of
selfish ambition,
worldly opinion,
 insecurity
and fear.

And when I hear,
may I be
bold to follow,
quick to answer,
completely in tune
with Your will.

Thank you, Father God.

You never leave me
nor forsake me.

You are always
right before me,
right behind me,
right beside me.

How blessed I am
to be Your child.

In Jesus' precious name,
I pray.

Amen.

Gracious Heavenly Father,

The sun
has yet to rise
and already
You have blessed me.

Safety through the night,
sleep that was sweet,
eyes that opened
to a brand new day,
and a heart spilling over
with praise for You.

Go with me
into this new day, Lord.

You are

The Way,

The Truth

 and The Life.

May my feet always
walk in Your way, Lord.

May my heart always
believe Your truth, Father.

May my life always
be a reflection of You, dear God.

This is the day
You have made.

How my heart
rejoices in it
and is glad.

In Jesus' precious name,
I pray.

Amen.

Gracious Heavenly Father,

How can I ever
begin to think,
You who created me
in my mother's womb –

sculpting my nose,

molding my frame,

choosing my eye color,

designing my mind,

developing my personality,

creating my very being,

would abandon
Your creative touch
in my life
once I am born?

Oh Father God,
So often,
I live my life
as though it is void
of Your presence.

I wonder about this
and I worry over that.

I try to figure out this situation
or determine that outcome.

I fear what I don't know
and I fear what I do know –

all the while,
carrying
regret and shame and guilt
like a ball and chain.

And,
I altogether
forget
this beautiful truth:

Life is not meant
to be spent in
fear or dread or regret,
but
in breathless anticipation
of what You are creating
in me,
through me,
in spite of me,
all around me.

You are Creator God.

In You,
all things have
their beginning
and their end.

And yet,
I forget to remember,
in You,
all things also have
their middle -
their very being,
their very existing.

You are
in every moment
of my life.

You are
forever using
your creative touch to

open a closed door,

bridge a gap,

provide a way,

mend a broken relationship,

soften a hardened heart,

heal a wound,

redeem a mistake,

transform a life.

From the
moment of conception,
until I take
my last and final breath,
You are forever
at work in my life.

Life is not meant
to be spent
in
fear or dread or regret,
but in
breathless anticipation
of what You are creating
in me,
through me,
in spite of me,
all around me.

You are Creator God,
and me,
I am the work
of Your creative touch -
each and every day
of my life.

In Jesus' precious name,
I pray.

Amen.

Gracious Heavenly Father,

May I this day,
not allow
my humanness,
my own feelings,
my own "take on things"
to take my thoughts
in a wrong direction.

May I not try
to second guess,
to pre-determine,
or pre-judge
those around me.

May I simply
live my life
as an instrument of your love -
giving grace,
taking no offense,
judging no one.

May I be
a peace maker,
love lavisher,
grace giver
everywhere I go,
to everyone I meet.

In Jesus' precious name,
I pray.

Amen.

Gracious Heavenly Father,

You are calling me
to move forward,
to step out
and take hold
of all that You
have promised me,
in and through
Christ Jesus,
Your son.

Joy.

Hope.

Peace.

Love.

Strength.

Comfort.

Forgiveness.

Mercy.

Grace.

Salvation.

All of these are
mine for the taking,
mine for the enjoying,
mine for the living,
mine for all eternity,
if - - -
I am willing,
in faith,

to step
out into them,

to possess
what You
have placed
before me,

to receive
what You
have already given.

Lord,
may I not be
like the ten spies

who ventured into
the Promised Land
only to
turn around
in fear and trembling.

May I not be
like these ten
and talk myself
out of
all that You
are calling
me to.

May I instead,
Father God,
be like Joshua and Caleb.

Instead of looking
at my giants,
may I look at You.

Instead of worrying
about defeat,
may I be
a warrior unto victory.

Instead of turning
back,
may I courageously
step forward.

May I not focus
on all that would
keep me
from living in
the land of Your blessings,
the place of Your promise.

May I instead,
focus on You,
and with
great excitement,
hopeful anticipation,
unwavering faith,
take hold
of all that You
have so graciously
placed before me.

In Jesus' precious name,
I pray.

Amen.

Gracious Heavenly Father,

As I step out
into a new day,
may the desire
of my heart
not be
to belong to the world,
but to belong to You.

May I not
break and bend
trying to fit
into the mold
of the world,
but may I instead,
allow my Spirit
and my heart
to be broken and molded
into the image
of You.

May I not
strive to
be like,
act like,
live like

those in the world
around me,
but may I instead,
be like,
act like,
live like
the very heart
of You.

I don't want to
"fit in"
to the world, Lord.

I want to
fit in to
Your plans,
Your will,
Your destiny.

I want You to
"fit me" for
kingdom work,
kingdom living,
Your kingdom to come.

Let me not look
at the world;
let me look at You.

In Jesus' precious name,
I pray.

Amen.

Gracious Heavenly Father,

I pray You
will be the
strength
of my life today.

In moments of
weakness,
weariness,
and "I wonder how I will"
be my strength.

In moments of
temptation,
tension,
and "I don't think I can"
be my strength.

In moments of
frustration,
fear,
and "I am overwhelmed"
be my strength.

You are Almighty God.

Nothing is too hard for You.

Nothing is
beyond Your ability,
beyond Your hand.

Nothing -
absolutely nothing -
can defeat me
when You are here.

Uphold me,
sustain me,
empower me.

Let me feel
Your strength
alive in me today.

Thank you, Lord.

In Jesus' precious name,
I pray.

Amen

Gracious Heavenly Father,

How patient
and persistent
You are.

To think
You love me enough
to continue
to work
this stubborn
lump of clay,
day after day after day,
totally amazes me.

To think
You would continue
to pick me up,
and start anew,
time and time and time again -
what love is this.

Lord,
 I've had enough
of being
 "me".

My heart long
to be
like You.

As painful
as it may be
to be made new
in You,
I surrender
to the work
of Your hands, Father.

Take me
and make me
into
Your image.

Take me
and mold me
into
that which
You created
me to be
before the foundations
of the world.

Take me
and make me

so the me
of who I am
is no longer
recognizable
and the You
of who You are
in me
is undeniable.

Mold.

Shape.

Design.

Squeeze.

Push.

Pull.

Whatever it takes, Lord.

In Jesus' precious name,
I pray.

Amen.

Gracious Heavenly Father,

To be so
in love
with You,
Jesus,
that pleasing You
above all else,
pleases me
above all else -
this,
this is the desire
of my heart.

This is the place
I long
for my heart
to discover.

Draw me unto You,
Father God.

Woo me
with Your precious
Holy Spirit.

May my heart
hear Yours

calling me
out of myself
and into You.

This is my prayer,
Father God.

In Jesus' precious name,
I pray.

Amen.

Gracious Heavenly Father,

May my heart,
my mind,
my very living
and breathing
be so filled
with You,
there will be
no room left

for compromise.

In Jesus' precious name,
I pray.

Amen.

Gracious Heavenly Father,

As I begin
a new day,
I give thanks
that YOU
are with me.

I need
Your wisdom
so I can know
the way
I should go.

I need
Your love and compassion
so I can be
Your hands,
Your feet,
Your embrace.

I need
Your Spirit
so I can control
my thoughts
and my tongue
and present
each word
I speak
as a gift.

I need
Your courage
so I can
step out in faith.
beyond
what I can see,
to where
You are calling me.

I need
Your presence,
in me,
working through me,
shining out of me.

Thank you, Father.

In Jesus' precious name,
I pray.

Amen.

Gracious Heavenly Father,

I come before You
with my heart
bowed
in adoration.

With the mere mention
of Your Son's name,
the precious name of Jesus,

I can

enter into Your presence,

receive Your forgiveness,

know Your companionship,

taste Your goodness,

invoke Your power.

With the mere mention
of Your Son's name,
the precious name of Jesus,

I can

survive any affliction,

loosen chains of addiction,

send demons running,

set captives free,

turn this world upside down.

Jesus.

Jesus.

Jesus –

the sweetest,
yet most powerful name
I can ever speak.

Thank you,
Father God,
for the gift
of Your Son.

Thank you
for the
difference
He makes
in my life
and through
my life.

How I praise You.

In the
mighty,
powerful,
beautiful,
precious
name of Jesus,
I pray.

Amen.

About the Author

Stacy is a seeker of God's heart.

Daily she is learning who she is
in and through Christ Jesus, her Lord.

She is a heart transformed by His love,
a life changed by His presence,
a sinner saved by His grace.

As she seeks
to know God more intimately,
through the ordinary,
day to day happenings of her life,
she marvels to discover
God is always faithful
to leave heartprints of His love
scattered across the pages
of her life story.

It is these heartprints
Stacy writes about on her blog,
"Heartprints of God",
and loves to speak about
at women's events.

It is the desire of Stacy's heart,
that through the sharing
of her own heartprint of God sightings,
others will start to see
heartprints of God
in their own lives
and be drawn ever closer to Him.

She prays
that as the Holy Spirit
speaks through something she writes,
or something she says,
others will find God,
and in doing so,
find the very heart
of who they are.

Stacy - a teacher of 18 years -
is currently a writer, and speaker.

Stacy is also the author of two other books:

If Only I Could:
A Journey of Loving,
Missing, and Living Beyond

You'll Be Fine, Beautiful. You've Got God:
Experiencing God in the Midst of Grief

Raw, intimate, honest and profound –
both are a poignant, personal journey
through grief and are available for purchase
on Amazon.

Connect with Stacy

Stacy loves recounting
God's faithfulness in her life
and sharing His heartprints.
For weekly heartprint sightings,
subscribe to her blog at
 www.heartprintsofgod.com

On social media follow Stacy on
Facebook, Instagram, and Twitter
at Heartprints of God.

Stacy is also available
to speak at women's events
and retreats.

If you're interested
in having her come
to your event
email Stacy at Stacy@StacyLSanchez.com

27447875R00069